B is for Bacon Tree
Bacon from A to Z

Written by
Harrison Martin

Illustrated by
M. T. Bear

Flipféóg Books

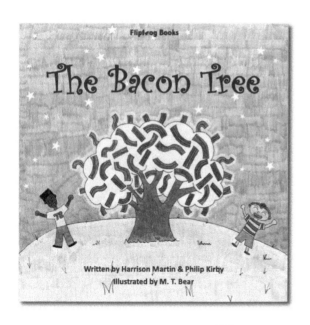

Flipfrog Books™ and [book logo]™ are registered trademarks of Flipfrog, LLC.
Published by Flipfrog Books, an endeavor of Flipfrog, LLC.
PO Box 273, Pfafftown, NC 27040
Text copyright © 2020 by Harrison Martin
Illustrations copyright © 2020 by M. T. Bear
Editing & Design by Jennifer Martin
Library of Congress Control Number: 2020924487
ISBN: 978-1-7923-4638-5 (Paperback)
www.flipfrogllc.com/flipfrogbooks

This book was typeset in Comic Sans and Curlz MT.
The illustrations were done in colored pencil, ink, and watercolor paint.

To my wonderful mother, Libby. Thank you for teaching me my ABC's and how to read and write. Without those fundamental skills I would not have written this book. – H.M.

To my wonderful nieces and nephews; Jade, Jaxon, Elijah, Jaeson, Ethan, Ean, Jai, and Jayla. Now you can tell people you have a book dedicated to you. – M.T.B.

This book belongs to

Hey there, I'm the bacon tree!
Surely you remember me?
Whether breakfast, lunch or a snack for thee
You can always come to see... well me.

Now I'll tell you something very neat.
I think you'll consider it a nifty treat.
Hear me now and feel free to repeat.
There are DIFFERENT bacons that you can eat!

I tell you now that it's a fact.
Not something that I will retract.
Don't believe me? Just come and see.
I'll show you bacon from A to Z.

A is for Applewood Smoked Bacon

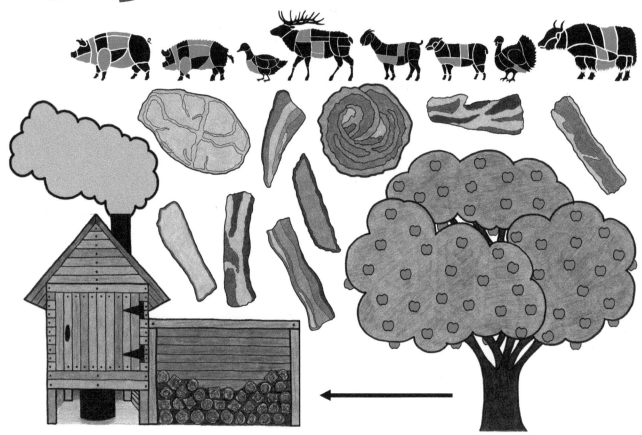

This bacon has been smoked with applewood, giving the meat a light, fruity, and slightly sweet aroma and taste.

B is for Back Bacon

This comes from the fat back or the loin of the pig. A butcher can also cut pork chops from pork loin.

C is for Candied Bacon

This is made by coating thick strips of bacon in caramel, honey, molasses, chocolate or sugar (notably brown sugar). Spices and nuts can be added for extra flavor.

D is for Duck Bacon

This lower-fat alternative to pork bacon is cut from very thick slices of duck breast. It has more flavor and better texture than turkey bacon.

E is for Elk Bacon

This is made from Elk bellies and shoulders.
It is cured before smoking for flavor.

F is for Frühstücksspeck

This is smoked or pickled pork belly with or without some meat in it.
Frühstücksspeck means "breakfast speck" in German.

G is for Gypsy Bacon

RIND

This is cured with the rind (skin) still on and is best cooked over an open flame.
Beneath the rind are layers of meat and fat, each layer between 1/4 inch to 1/2 inch thick.

H is for Hickory Smoked Bacon

This bacon has been smoked with hickory chips that give the meat a smokey southern aroma and taste.

I is for Imaginary Bacon

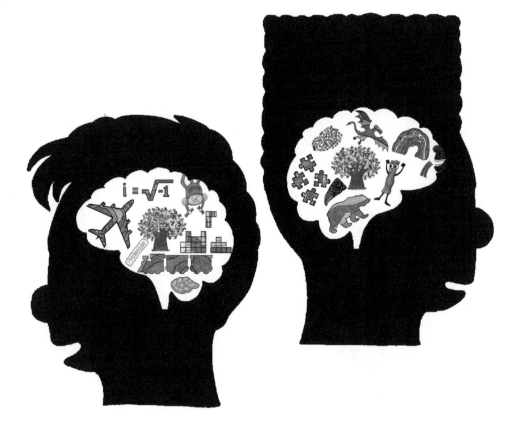

This is different types, shapes, and colors of bacon that fill your thoughts and dreams when you can't eat bacon at that very moment.

J is for Jowl Bacon

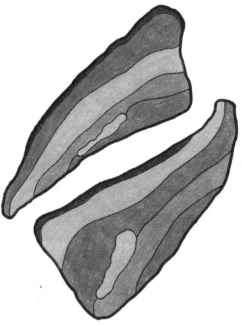

This is cured and smoked cheeks of pork.

In Italy, Guanciale is a jowl bacon that is seasoned and dry cured but not smoked.

K is for Kunekune Bacon

This is made from the kunekune, a small breed of domestic pig from New Zealand.
This bacon is dark and rich in flavor and nutrients.

L is for Lardons

This is small strips or cubes of bacon or pork fat used in a variety of cuisines to flavor salads and savory foods.

M is for Macon

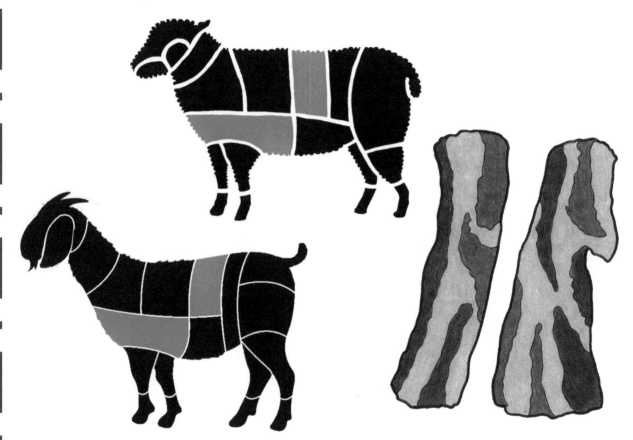

A portmanteau of the words mutton and bacon. This is cured and smoked from mutton (sheep or goat meat).

N is for New Zealand Bacon

This comes from the New Zealand pork industry. They don't use any growth hormones and the use of antibiotics is strictly controlled. Sows are farmed outdoors in paddocks with shelter to protect them from the elements and huts for breeding.

O is for Orange-Glazed Bacon

This type of candied bacon is coated in a glaze made from orange juice and honey.

P is for Pancetta

This Italian form of side bacon, available smoked or unsmoked, is generally rolled up into cylinders after curing and is known for having a strong flavor.

Q is for Quality Bacon

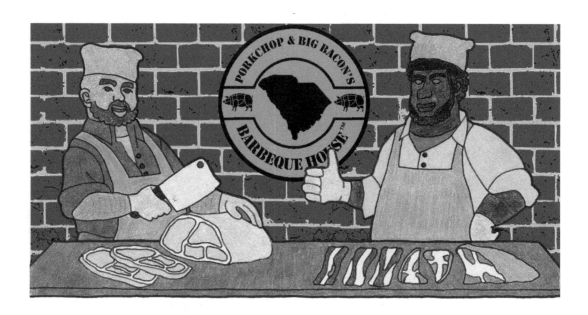

The best quality bacon comes straight from the butcher. It has fewer preservatives. It can be purchased in slabs of any cut and to a thickness of your preference. Center cut is recommended for its greater meat to fat ratio.

R is for Rasher

This leaner, meatier thin slice of bacon is common in the United Kingdom and Ireland.

S is for Szalonna

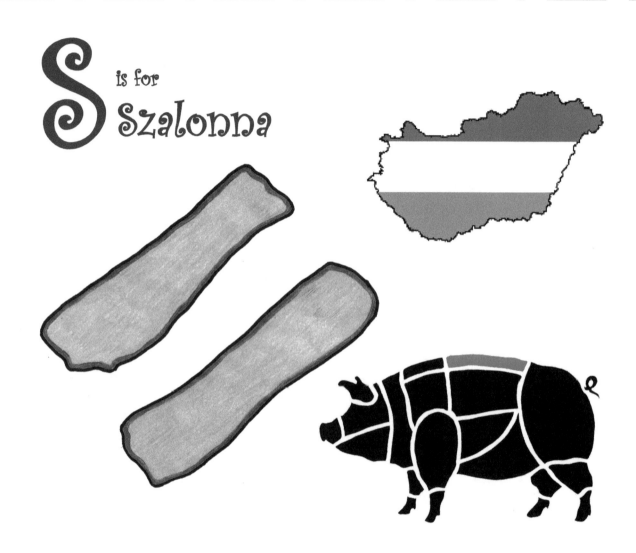

This is a Hungarian variety of pork fatback that is often smoked or cooked before purchase so that the buyer can eat it without further preparation.

T is for Turkey Bacon

This lower-fat alternative to pork bacon is prepared from smoked turkey. It is a practical alternative in cultures where eating pork is forbidden.

(This is not available from the bacon tree.)

U is for Uncured Bacon

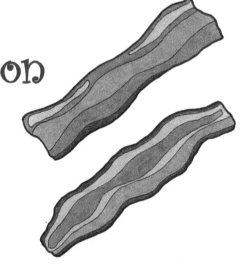

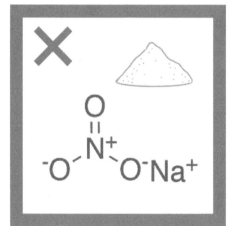

Technically considered a misnomer, uncured bacon is cured with natural nitrites (beet extract, sea salt, celery salt, and parsley) instead of sodium nitrites.

V is for Vegan Bacon

An alternative to animal-based bacon, this can be made from a variety of plants and fungi including: carrots, coconuts, soybeans, seaweed, seitan, and mushrooms.

W is for Woven Bacon

This is slices of bacon woven together in a square or rectangular lattice and cooked for use on sandwiches.

X is for Xanthic Bacon

Xanthic is an adjective meaning of or relating to a yellow or yellowish color. Peameal bacon (from Canada) is xanthic because it is coated in fine-ground cornmeal (historically, it was rolled in ground, dried yellow peas).

Y is for Yak Bacon

This is made from fatty pieces of yak (long-haired domesticated cattle) found in the Himalayan region.

Z is for Zesty Bacon

Zesty is an adjective meaning to have a strong, pleasant, and somewhat spicy flavor. This can be made by adding a variety of seasonings to the bacon before cooking.

Now wasn't that very neat
To see all that delicious meat?
Read it backwards and then you can say,
"I know bacon from Z to A."

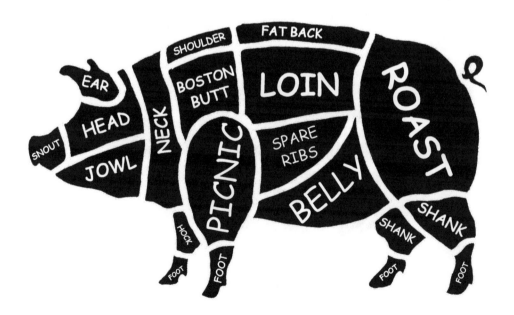

CPSIA information can be obtained
at www.ICGtesting.com
Printed in the USA
BVHW020338080121
597086BV00003B/52